92
Carver
G. W.

10047

Towne, Peter.
    George Washington Carver / by Peter
Towne [i.e. P. Nabokov] ; illustrated
by Elzia Moon. New York : Crowell,
[1975]
    32 p. : ill. (some col.) ; 24 cm. (A
Crowell biography)
    A simple biography of the Negro
scientist famed for his revolutionary
agricultural research.


    1. Carver, George Washington, 1864?-
1943.  2. Scientists.  3. Afro-
Americans--Biography.  I. Moon, Elzia,
ill.  II. Title

# GEORGE WASHINGTON CARVER

# GEORGE WASHINGTON CARVER

## By Peter Towne
## Illustrated by Elzia Moon

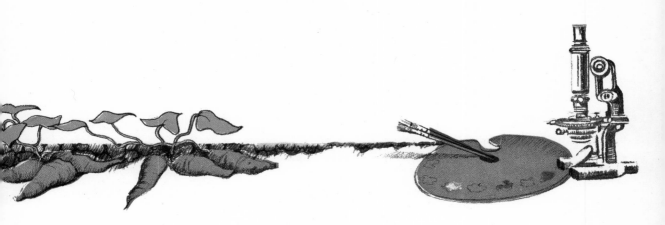

Thomas Y. Crowell Company
New York

## CROWELL BIOGRAPHIES
### Edited by Susan Bartlett Weber

JANE ADDAMS *by Gail Faithfull Keller*

MARIAN ANDERSON *by Tobi Tobias*

LEONARD BERNSTEIN *by Molly Cone*

MARTHA BERRY *by Mary Kay Phelan*

GEORGE WASHINGTON CARVER
*by Peter Towne*

WILT CHAMBERLAIN *by Kenneth Rudeen*

RAY CHARLES *by Sharon Bell Mathis*

CESAR CHAVEZ *by Ruth Franchere*

SAMUEL CLEMENS
*by Charles Michael Daugherty*

ROBERTO CLEMENTE *by Kenneth Rudeen*

CHARLES DREW *by Roland Bertol*

FANNIE LOU HAMER *by June Jordan*

LANGSTON HUGHES, AMERICAN POET
*by Alice Walker*

JAMES WELDON JOHNSON
*by Ophelia Settle Egypt*

FIORELLO LA GUARDIA
*by Mervyn Kaufman*

THE MAYO BROTHERS *by Jane Goodsell*

ARTHUR MITCHELL *by Tobi Tobias*

JOHN MUIR *by Charles P. Graves*

JESSE OWENS *by Mervyn Kaufman*

GORDON PARKS *by Midge Turk*

ROSA PARKS *by Eloise Greenfield*

THE RINGLING BROTHERS *by Molly Cone*

PAUL ROBESON *by Eloise Greenfield*

JACKIE ROBINSON *by Kenneth Rudeen*

ELEANOR ROOSEVELT *by Jane Goodsell*

MARIA TALLCHIEF *by Tobi Tobias*

JIM THORPE *by Thomas Fall*

THE WRIGHT BROTHERS
*by Ruth Franchere*

MALCOLM X *by Arnold Adoff*

*Library of Congress Cataloging in Publication Data.* ———. George Washington Carver. SUMMARY: A simple biography of the Negro scientist famed for his revolutionary agricultural research. 1. Carver, George Washington, 1864?–1943—Juv. lit. [1. Carver, George Washington, 1864?–1943. 2. Scientists. 3. Negroes—Biography] I. Moon, Elzia, ill. II. Title. S417.C3N32 630'.92'4 [B] 74-34296 ISBN 0-690-00776-0 ISBN 0-690-00777-9 (lib. bdg.)

1 2 3 4 5 6 7 8 9 10

# GEORGE WASHINGTON CARVER

CB A CROWELL BIOGRAPHY

George Washington Carver lived to be an old and famous scientist. But when he was born around 1860 his mother Mary was afraid he wouldn't live a day longer. He was so thin and sickly. She gave him just one name—George.

Mary was a black woman who belonged to a white farmer named Moses Carver. For a long time some white people in America had been

buying and selling black people. The black people were called slaves. They were used like work animals.

Moses Carver thought it was wrong to own slaves the way he owned his plow horses. But his wife wanted help with the housework. So for $700 Mr. Carver had bought Mary when she was thirteen years old.

The moment George was born he also belonged to Mr. Carver. He was known as Carver's George.

Mary had many troubles. Two of her children had died as babies. Shortly before George's birth his father was killed in an accident. And little George coughed so badly that Mary had to give him spoonfuls of honey

1

water mixed with a wild leaf called tansy. Then he breathed more easily.

Something else was worrying Mary. There was a terrible war in America, called the Civil War. People from the south of the country were fighting hard for the right to keep their slaves. The northern people said that was wrong. Mr. Carver's farm lay outside of Diamond Grove, Missouri, between the North and South. Men called night riders used the war as an excuse to steal slaves and sell them again.

One night some horsemen broke into Mary's cabin. They grabbed her and the small baby in her arms.

2

Moses Carver sent a man to find the night riders. He never did find Mary. But one day he stopped at a farmhouse. A baby, ill with whooping cough, had been abandoned there by the horsemen. It was George.

Susan Carver nursed George back to health. But all that coughing injured George's throat. As he grew up, people were surprised at his high-pitched voice. He sort of chirped, they said, like a bird.

People were also surprised at something else about George. He learned very quickly. He would watch Susan Carver knit and say, "I can do that." Then he would pick up the knitting needles and use them perfectly.

George was a shy boy who liked to be alone. He never was very strong or handsome. As he grew, his back became bent and his arms were long and thin. But George had that special gift for learning things on his own.

He used to watch Susan Carver sweep the house, wash clothes, make medicines from herbs and barks. He watched Moses Carver tan hides, sew shoes, and cure bacon. He listened to people sing in church. All the time he said, "I can do that." And he usually could.

When George wasn't weeding the garden or milking cows he would wander into the woods. There he picked up wild flowers, weeds, and bugs. He also liked to collect rocks, feathers, and leaves.

George kept a secret garden in the woods where he grew plants. Soon he could tell when his flowers needed water and when they needed sunlight. He made colors from mashed berries and roots and painted pictures with them.

George was always asking himself questions. Why do roots that look the same grow into plants with different-colored flowers? What happens to the white fluff that pops out of milkweed pods when you open them?

Neighbors asked Susan Carver why she had the prettiest roses around. "It's all because of George," she explained. "He has a magic way with growing things." Even when he was ten years old, George was known as "the Plant Doctor."

But he was anxious to learn more than the Carvers could teach him. By now the Civil War was over. It had been won by the North and slaves were supposed to be free. George asked Mr. Carver if he could go to the school nearby. Mr. Carver had to tell him that it was only for white children.

George felt sure he could learn anything if only he had the chance. Then he heard about a

school for black children in Neosho, Missouri.
"I am going there," he told the Carvers.

Early one morning George dressed in his
Sunday suit. He tied some corn bread, his
favorite rocks and feathers, and a clean shirt
into a bandanna. Then he walked the eight
miles to the Lincoln School for Colored Children.

That first night in the strange town George
slept in a barn. In the morning he found the
school building but its doors were locked.
George sat down on the steps.

"What are you doing there?" a black
woman asked.

"I'm waiting for school to open," answered
George.

She smiled. "It's Sunday. There's no school today. Tomorrow you can go." Her name was Mariah Watkins. She invited George to stay with her and her husband Andy for a while.

On Monday morning George started school at last. Seventy-five children sat on hard benches in the one-room cabin. In wintertime they had to wear coats and mittens indoors because there was no heat. George learned fast there, even though he was often sick.

Mrs. Watkins was a washerwoman. George called her Aunt Mariah. At night she showed him how to wash and iron clothes and how to sew and crochet. On Sundays she took him to the African Methodist Church. George loved to sing the gospel songs.

One day Aunt Mariah told him, "You can't go calling yourself Carver's George anymore. You're a free man. From now on you're going to be George Carver."

At Christmas George gave Aunt Mariah a dress he had crocheted for her. She gave him a Bible. For the rest of his life George read from that Bible every day and took it to church with him every Sunday.

Aunt Mariah could tell when George had learned all the Lincoln school had to offer. He kept asking questions no one could answer. She did not try to stop him when he began to look for another school somewhere else.

George was thirteen years old when he again packed his few belongings. He was sad

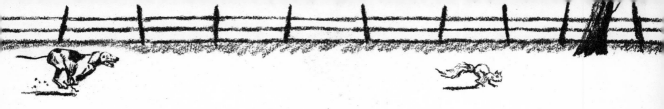

to leave Aunt Mariah. She had given him a warm and loving home.

George caught a wagon ride with a family to Fort Scott, Kansas, seventy-five miles away. He found many different jobs there. Whenever he saved enough money, he attended school for a few months.

One day in Fort Scott some white men stopped George in the street and beat him because he was black. They stole his precious school books. Soon after, George saw a black man burned to death by some other white men. It frightened him so much he left Fort Scott the next morning.

For ten years George wandered from place to place, going to school whenever he could. He was quiet and did not talk to people very much. For money he cooked, chopped wood, washed clothes, dug ditches, and painted

fences. He was glad when he could weed
gardens or harvest crops. George still had his
love of plants and growing things.

In Minneapolis, Kansas, George heard
about another man who had exactly the same
name as he did—George Carver. He decided
to use "W" for a middle initial so people
could tell them apart. George W. Carver, he
wrote.

12

"Does the W. mean Washington?" someone asked. "Why not?" George answered.

After graduation from high school in Minneapolis George felt ready for college. He went to Highland University in Kansas to enroll.

"I'm George W. Carver, sir," George said to the principal. "I've come to start college."

The principal looked at him with cold eyes. "We don't take niggers here," he said.

George felt angry and hurt as he walked away. But he did not fight back. Instead he moved again, this time to the Kansas frontier where there was free land for settlers who would farm it. There he lived by himself on his own little farm until he heard about a college that accepted blacks.

"What are those for?" a friend asked as George put some crochet designs in the bag he was packing for college.

"I'm going South to my people some day," George answered quietly. "And I expect to use these designs to teach them what they can make with their own hands."

This was the first time George had ever told anyone about his dream of helping black people.

George was twenty-six years old when he entered Simpson College in Indianola, Iowa. He had waited a long time for this opportunity.

Since he was black he was not allowed to live with the white students. To earn money for food he set up a laundry business and washed other students' clothes. Once a friend visited George's tiny cabin. George was scrubbing clothes, eating his homemade soup, and reading a book—all at the same time.

George did so well at Simpson that his

teachers urged him to make agriculture—the art of growing good crops—and botany—the study of plant life—his life's work. They suggested he study at the Iowa State College of Agriculture at Ames.

At Ames George worked with the best professors in agricultural science. He began to understand how plants receive minerals from the soil the way a person's body gets vitamins from food. He learned how the soil must get back those minerals through manures and fertilizers.

George became interested in crossbreeding plants. He put pollen from one plant on the flower of a different kind of plant and got seed for a new kind. Crossbreeding could add new colors to flowers. It could also make new fruits for people to eat.

George was very pleased when the college

asked him to become a teacher. He was the first black man to graduate from the school. Now he would be its first black teacher.

George's next two years at Ames were happy. He was very popular with his students. They called him Professor Carver. He was put in charge of the school greenhouse. He wrote articles about one of the kinds of diseases that can kill plants—a field of study called mycology.

Still George held to his dream of helping his own people. But where in the South could he help most? Then George received a letter from a man named Booker T. Washington.

Dr. Washington had also started life as a slave. He had gone to school at Hampton Institute in Virginia. Hampton was the first school to help young blacks to make a living as free men and women. Its motto was "Learn by doing."

In 1881 Dr. Washington opened his own school in Tuskegee, Alabama. It had the same goal, "Learn by doing." Dr. Washington wanted the Tuskegee students to learn to support themselves. Even if blacks and whites had to live separately, he said, young black people first of all needed the knowledge and skills to look after themselves.

Other black leaders disagreed with Dr. Washington. They thought their people should fight first for their rights to live and work and go to school wherever they wanted.

In his letter Dr. Washington invited George to teach agriculture at his school in Tuskegee. Right away George said yes. This was exactly what he had been looking for.

But it was hard to say good-bye to Ames. His friends gave him a microscope as a farewell present. George left to the school his collection of plants.

It was a long train ride from Iowa to Alabama. As the train rattled south George watched the farmland change. The rich brown earth of the prairie gave way to reddish Alabama clay.

George saw black men and women bent over low, green cotton plants. They were filling long sacks with the puffy white balls of cotton. He thought, there is the reason I am going to Dr. Washington's school. Black people need a chance for something better in life than picking another man's crop for a few cents. And that worn-out red Alabama soil needs a rest from cotton growing.

When George arrived at Tuskegee he saw only one brick building and a few old cabins. The ground was bare of grass. "What do you think of our school?" Dr. Washington asked him.

"There seems much to be done," George answered.

George was given thirteen students to teach. First, we need a laboratory, he told them. At the school's junk heap the students collected old bottles, rusty pans, fruit jar tops, bits of wire. They cleaned up a dirty oil lamp to provide light for George's new microscope. A teacup with a broken handle became a grinder for breaking up seeds and mashing berries. They punched holes in pieces of tin to make a strainer.

At his direction the boys brought back buckets of rotten leaves and swamp muck from the woods. They dumped them into a hole to make what George called a compost heap. Over the fall and winter they added potato peelings, egg shells, and other garbage. They were making their own fertilizer.

By spring the compost was ready for the students to spread over their twenty acres of land. George explained that the compost gave the land back its minerals. Their first crop would need those minerals to grow.

But George had a new idea for that first crop, too. No cotton, he said. His boys were surprised. Cotton was all their parents had ever grown. Instead they would plant cowpeas, George told them, because cowpeas put nitrogen back into the soil. And nitrogen was important to healthy plants.

"A plant needs certain food," George explained to his students. "The ground has certain food to give plants. The good farmer just has to keep a balance between them."

After the first harvest of cowpeas George invited his students to dinner. They ate what they thought were delicious pancakes, potatoes, and meat loaf. When they finished George told them a secret. Everything had been made from mashed cowpeas. That was how George taught—he showed.

But teaching was only one of George's activities. He wrote a book that helped other teachers interest their students in botany. He wrote bulletins that showed people how to farm better and raise healthier cattle, pigs, and sheep. He painted pictures of flowers as a hobby, and he sang in the school choir. George was always busy.

Many black farmers around Tuskegee began coming to Professor George Carver for advice. He tested the drinking water in their

wells to make sure it was free from germs. He tried to persuade them to plant other crops besides cotton. But they told him that cotton was the only crop they could sell quickly for money to buy food for their families.

George and Dr. Washington often took walks together and shared their problems. When George said he wanted to start a school for farm families, Dr. Washington told him to go ahead.

George called this school the Farmer's Institute. In Tuskegee's dairy barn he showed the families how to feed their cows so they would give more milk. He offered to test their soil so they would know what fertilizer to use. Grow your own vegetables, he suggested, instead of buying them at the store. George told them how to raise chickens, how to make their own clothes and cook new kinds of dishes.

Still George felt this was not enough. So he built a wagon school pulled by a mule which he could drive to the farmers' homes. His wagon school held farm tools, seeds, soil samples, fertilizers, and George's own grown vegetables. He explained to farmers that tomatoes were not poisonous, as they thought, but good to eat. He showed how compost heaps could provide free fertilizer to grow bigger melons and larger cabbages. He looked at gardens and

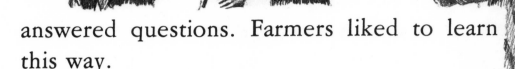

answered questions. Farmers liked to learn this way.

In 1898 the first Farmer's Institute fair was held at Tuskegee. People brought their prize fruits and vegetables, preserved food in jars, and their best barnyard animals.

George cooked his own soybean recipes for all to taste. He also showed the coffee, sugar, and laundry starch he had made from sweet potatoes. After that the fair was held each year.

Tuskegee had many students now and some fine new buildings. Wealthy white people who liked Dr. Washington's ideas gave him money for his school. They agreed that black and white people should help each other but not live together. This made other black leaders angry. They felt Dr. Washington was not helping blacks in the right way. George tried to stay out of this argument.

Then, suddenly, farmers throughout the South had an emergency. Everywhere a small insect called the boll weevil was eating up the cotton. Burn your infected cotton plants, George told them, and grow sweet potatoes, cowpeas, and peanut vines instead.

But who will buy all the peanuts you tell us to grow? the farmers asked George. In Alabama people sometimes ate peanuts, but no one used them for anything else.

As usual George was determined to find an answer. In his laboratory he mashed peanuts, cooked them, boiled them, strained them, and dried them. He pressed oil from them and beat their shells into fibers. He found that he could make peanut oil, peanut butter, peanut milk, peanut flour, and five kinds of peanut soup.

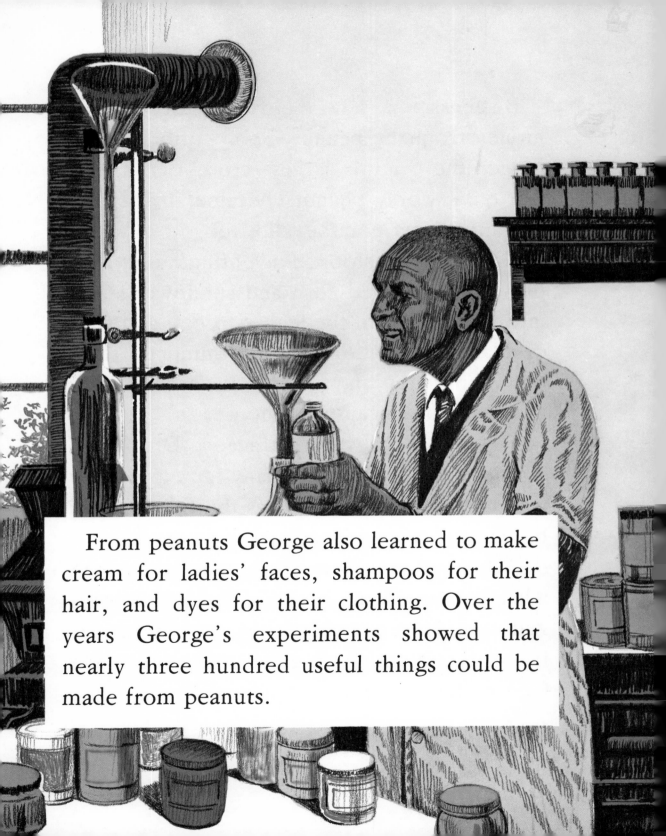

From peanuts George also learned to make cream for ladies' faces, shampoos for their hair, and dyes for their clothing. Over the years George's experiments showed that nearly three hundred useful things could be made from peanuts.

Businessmen saw that they could make money from the peanut. Soon cotton was no longer the South's largest crop. Because of George's work, peanuts became just as important. Sweet potatoes did, too.

George never stopped inventing ways to use plants. He pressed corn and sunflower stalks into boards. From the leaves, roots, and fruit of plants he made over five hundred cloth dyes. From the clay he dug up around Tuskegee he made paints for houses.

Then Tuskegee had a tragedy. Dr. Washington died. Among the many famous people who came to the funeral was the President of the United States, Theodore Roosevelt.

"There is no more important work than what you are doing here," President Roosevelt told George when they met. With his friend Dr. Washington gone, that work made George feel better.

Now George's name was well known. He was called the "Wizard of Tuskegee." Young scientists wanted to work with him in his laboratory. Visitors from many countries came to ask him questions. Henry Ford, the inventor of the Ford automobile, often stayed at Tuskegee to consult with George.

But none of this attention changed George. He remained a quiet and shy person. Every day he worked in floppy old pants that were stained with plant juices and chemicals. And every day he put a fresh flower in his buttonhole.

Usually George did not like to leave his work to meet guests. But if a visitor asked him something about a plant, a painting, a piece of music, or a selection from the Bible, his eyes would light up. He would start talking excitedly in his high voice.

In 1943 George Washington Carver died. He was eighty-two years old and had been at Tuskegee for over half his life. He was still earning just $125 a month—the same salary he had been given when he first went there.

On the Tuskegee school grounds a George Washington Carver Museum had been built. George had prepared the exhibits himself. They show how the earth's products can help mankind. The museum is also a history of George's life and work at Tuskegee.

Its walls are hung with George's beautiful flower paintings. Its cases display the many products George invented from cotton and peanuts and sweet potatoes. Behind the museum is the small greenhouse where George spent his last days caring for his plants.

In the years since 1943 black people have fought hard for the right to live and work and go to school wherever they wish. Some feel that George Carver was a black man who was afraid to fight for equality. But fighting back had never been George's way. He had always been a loner. His way of helping black people had been to show them how to help themselves.

## About the Author

Peter Towne is a young writer who lives in California. He became deeply interested in the many-sided genius of George Washington Carver while he was pursuing research in the field of his major interest, ethnic literature.

## About the Artist

Elzia Moon grew up in Maryland, Virginia, and Washington, D.C.; his boyhood familiarity with the country and people of Carver's life may account in part for the rich and evocative drawings in this book. Mr. Moon is also an accomplished fine artist, who has exhibited his paintings in this country, France, and Canada. He has lived in New York City ever since attending the Pratt Institute there.